W9-AEP-306

Poets of the Pacific

SECOND SERIES

Poets of the Pacific

SECOND SERIES

EDITED BY

YVOR WINTERS

Granger Index Reprint Series

BOOKS FOR LIBRARIES PRESS
FREEPORT, NEW YORK

A good many of these poems have appeared in the
following periodicals: *Factotum, The Hudson Review,
The New Mexico Quarterly Review, Poetry* (a maga-
zine of verse), and *Tomorrow*. Acknowledgment is
due the editors of these periodicals for permission to
republish.

Table of Contents

Introductory Note

In 1937 I published a small anthology of verse entitled *Twelve Poets of the Pacific*. This book contained poems by my wife, by Clayton Stafford, by Howard Baker, by myself, and by eight of my students and former students, among them J. V. Cunningham, Don Stanford, and Ann Stanford. The present collection is a kind of sequel, in that it contains, so far as my judgment and information will guide me, the best poets to appear at Stanford since 1937.

This is not an anthology of undergraduate poets, though two undergraduates appear in it. The contributors range in age from about twenty years to thirty-four. Of the men contributing, one was too young to be involved in the war, one served through the war in the merchant marine, the remainder served in various branches of the armed forces. Four of the men are married, one is the father of three children, and one the father of two. Two of the women are married. One of the men is now teaching at Colorado State College; two are engaged in business; two of the women are secretaries; one man and one woman are undergraduates at Stanford; the other contributors are graduate students at Stanford or elsewhere. The collection contains the work of people who, whatever their talents, are fairly mature and have seen something of the world. Two of the poets included in this volume, Pearce Young and Edgar Bowers, have been recipients of fellowships in creative writing, given by Dr. Edward Jones, in connection with the recent establishment of the Creative Writing Center at Stanford.

Because of the relative maturity of most of these poets, I have endeavored to exercise my editorial authority with a certain laxness. I have chosen the poets and also the poems, but I have included a certain amount of work with which I am not wholly in sympathy in order to give the poets a reasonably free opportunity to exhibit their own tastes and directions. The book seems to me a good one, nevertheless, or I would not trouble myself with it; and I believe that it contains a few poets, at least, who will make distinguished names for themselves.

YVOR WINTERS

Stanford University, 1949

RICHARD K. ARNOLD

Revolving doors have trapped our nervous feet,
And circling in a scheme to imitate
The hearts of clocks that tell us it is late,
They tick us off, like seconds, in the street.

Time, time, to turn the dial and hear the news;
To bolt the supper, see the picture show;
To drink the drink and think of long ago,
When emptiness was not so hard to lose.

The bar, the bus are filled with brusque intent.
The night's impellent hours will require
A ruthless verve and nerves of copper wire,
The adult's poise, the child's astonishment.

EIGHT O'CLOCK

Our coffee cups contain the litter
Of weekday morning darkness haste.
The breakfast leaves incisive bitter
Cohabitating with our taste.

The morning paper adds its flavor
To phantasies of rumor's slaves.
The print cannot afford to waver,
For order's what the dreamer craves.

Our office doors extend a greeting
With cold and stubby hands of brass.
At eight, the captives start competing,
Exhibited within the glass.

EDGAR BOWERS

VENUS

Her constant gesture spanned the air,
And constant eyes befogged our eyes
Whose guilty cast and devious stare
Sought knowledge in a vain surmise,

For all about her, nature rose
In harmony with our distress,
But in her face profound repose,
A surety profounder, yes,

Than any promised us by them
Who measure life for measure's sake.
(Forgetting their own secret phlegm,
They measure error by mistake.)

With caution and with small belief
That in her posture we should find
More than she showed us, constant grief,
More than we showed her, constant mind,

We moved within her gesture's space.
Then marble grew our bones and flesh
And from the head to line the face
Came brain's entangled, mended mesh.

I

The fierce and brooding holocaust of faith
This people conquered, which no edict could,
And wove its spirit stiff and rich like cloth
That many years ago was soaked in blood.

Their minds are active only in their hands
To check and take the labor of the hills,
To furnish nature its precise demands
And bear its harshness as it seems God wills.

But holy passion hurts them in each season
To blend themselves with nature if they can;
They find in well known change enough of reason
To worship Him in it as Him in Man.

Thus in the summer on the Alpine heights
A deity of senseless wrath and scorn
Is feasted through the equinoctial nights
As though a savage Christ were then reborn.

Up from the floors of churches in December
The passion rises to a turbulence
Of darkness such as threatens to dismember
The mind submerged in bestial innocence.

And Druid shades with old dementia fraught
Possess the souls they had accounted loss
And join their voices raging and distraught
About the curious symbol of the cross.

II

I know a wasted place high in the Alps
Called Witches' Kitchen. There the sun all day
With aberrant change of shadows plagues the eyes,
And when the equinoctial moon has play

Upon the beast-like monoliths of stone,
The blood runs cold as its old passions rise
To haunt the memory of what we are
And what we do in worshipping brute skies.

Below this waste of spirit and of mind
The village Holy Blood with ordered care
Was founded on deep meadows. Yearly, sheep
Are brought to graze in summer pastures there.

Its people sow and harvest grain together
Between the comings of the winters' ice,
And when they stop to take a quick sprung flower
Its being and their gesture will suffice

To balance what they are and what are not.
And if we turn to look within the town
Upon a wall we find the stencilled group
Of Mary, John and others taking down

The body of their Master from the tree.
And just at dusk the daylight's weakened pace
Shades the blue chalk of Mary's robe with red;
And her faint tears are red upon His face.

This is the freezing guilt I shall remember
That I would mourn for Him I cannot know:
As if the loss of some life-giving member
Had doomed Him as a seasonal man of snow.

Against each perfect note I bear all thought.
Before the passion of thy complex grace
Flesh melts from bone that lies across the face,
And thought lies bare to what thy genius wrought.

But thought to most with faint acceptance blames
Who find no human feeling in such form;
And the desire that rhetoric perform
Its unique cries I counter with no claims

But say that in Saalfelden once I played
Upon thine own clavier, now black with age,
Some remnant of thy sweet and decorous rage
Until such condescending minds, afraid

To cant against such naked elegance,
Could speak no more of spectacular innocence.

The hovering and huge, dark, formless sway
That nature moves by laws we contemplate
We name for lack of name as order, fate,
God, principle, or primum mobile.
But in that graven image, word made wood
By skillful faith of him to whom she was
Eternal nature, first and final cause,
The form of knowledge knowledge understood
Bound human thought against the dark we find:
And body took the image of the mind
To shape in chaos a congruent form
Of will and matter, equal, side by side,
Upon the act of faith, within the norm
Of carnal being, blind and glorified.

With their harsh leaves old rhododendrons fill
The crevices in grave plots' broken stones.
The bees renew the blossoms they destroy,
While in the burning air the pines rise still,
Commemorating long forgotten biers,
Whose roots replace the semblance of these bones.

The weight of cool, of imperceptible dust
That came from nothing and to nothing came
Is light within the earth and on the air.
The change that so renews itself is just.
The enormous, sundry platitude of death
Is for these bones, bees, trees, and leaves the same.

And splayed upon the ground and through the trees
The mountains' shadow fills and cools the air,
Smoothing the shape of headstones to the earth.
The rhododendrons suffer with the bees
Whose struggles loose ripe petals to the earth,
The heaviest burden it shall ever bear.

Our hard earned knowledge fits us for such sleep.
Although the spring must come, it passes too
To form the burden suffered for what comes.
Whatever we would give our souls to keep
Is only part of what we call the soul;
What we of time would threaten to undo

All time in its slow scrutiny has done.
For on the grass that starts about the feet
The body's shadow turns, to shape in time,
Soon grown preponderant with creeping shade,
The final shadow that is turn of earth;
And what seems won paid for as in defeat.

THE WISE MEN

Far to the east I see them in my mind
Coming in every year to that one place.
They carry in their hands what they must find,
In their own faces bare what they shall face.

They move in silence, permanent and sure,
Like figurines of porcelain set with gold,
The colors of their garments bright and pure,
Their graceful features elegant and old.

They do not change: nor war nor peace define
Nor end the journey that each year the same
Renders them thus. They wait upon the sign
That promises no future but their name.

Incredibly near the vital edge of tears
I write, Constanze, having heard our loss.
Only the shape of memory adheres
To the most nearly perfect human pose
I hope to find, though mind and heart grow fierce,
Five times again as fierce, as his repose.

The mind of most of us is trivial,
And heart is moved too quickly and too much.
He thought each movement that was animal,
And senses were the mind's continual search
To find the perfect note, emotional
And mental, each the other one's reproach.

With him as master, grief should be serene,
Death its own joy and joy opposed by death,
What is made living by what should have been
And understanding constant in its wrath
To fix within one's life them both the same,
Though no one can, unless it be in death.

Yet we who loved him have that right to mourn.
Let this be mine, that fastened on my eyes
I carry one small memory of his form
Aslant at his clavier with careful ease
To cast one last enigma on the norm,
Intelligence perfecting the mute keys.

The Stoic: *for Laura von Courten*

All winter long you listened for the boom
Of distant cannon wheeled into their place.
Sometimes outside beneath a bombers' moon
You stood alone to watch the searchlights trace

Their careful webs against the boding sky,
While miles away on Munich's vacant square
The bombs lunged down with an unruly cry
Whose blast you saw yet could but faintly hear.

And might have turned your eyes upon the gleam
Of a thousand years' of snow where near the clouds
The Alps ride massive to their full extreme,
And season after season glacier crowds

The dark persistent smudge of conifers.
Or seen beyond the hedge and through the trees
The shadowy forms of cattle on the furze,
Their dim coats white with mist against the freeze.

Or thought instead of other times than these,
Of other countries and of other sights:
Eternal Venice sinking by degrees
Into the very water that she lights;

Reflected in canals, the lucid dome
Of Maria del Salute at your feet,
Her triple spires disfigured by the foam.
Remembered in Berlin the parks, the neat

Footpaths and lawns, the clean spring foliage
Where just short weeks ago a bomb unaimed
Had freed a raging lion from its cage
Which in the mottled dark that trees enflamed

Killed one who hurried homeward from the raid.
And by yourself there standing in the chill
You must, with so much known, have been afraid
And chosen such a mind of constant will,

Which though all time corrode with constant hurt
Remains until it occupies no space
That which it is; and passionless, inert,
Becomes at last no meaning and no place.

FRANCES CRAWFORD

I

The subtle evil that the mind engenders,
Projection of self, penumbra of decay,
Invisible in its parent, but manifest
In deeds; no force of the unhealthy heart
Has strength except in malice; only faith
Protects the poisoner from his own wine.
And if we have no fetishes, no faith,
No turning to future heaven, but doomed to hell,
No recourse to Rhadamanthus' judgment stays
The prejudged punishment enforced on self.
Only dark Phlegethon keeps to its course,
Preventing by its fires return to earth.

II

Who comforts flesh unreconciled,
The spirit begging to be bound?
Leave space, destroy the flesh reviled,
The interval recalls no sound.

The hand that holds no instrument
Cannot create, impatient god.
How can the unarmed have intent?
Even the wrathful bears a rod.

Bodiless soul cannot perceive.
Then can the eyeless find their way?
The huddled spirit fears to leave,
Corruption near, it dares not stay.

III

Uncaptured is essential death,
Free is its visitation,
In aspect like the humid breath,
Visible in occurence.

IV

It is a secret sorrow
To see the black squirrel,
Sun-glossed, impersonally
Existing in circumstance.

V

Intensity abstracted in air, ready to break
In fragmentation of despair;
Distortion of experience, immediate and informed
Of an impossible fulfillment;

Released to discomfort and vague speech of commonplace
Concealing the fact of sorrow,
Minor contortions of the concrete mind, returning
To hateful equilibrium.

The statement is here, the act attempted, unaccomplished,
And between the desire and deed,
The painful void, diminishing, intensifies
Until the wound is scarred by forgetting.

VI

The supple body bends to will
And then springs back like sapling tree
Or like the grass behind the wind
Erect, free from identity.

It has no need of subtle mind
For simple want and quick desire.
With longing satisfied, it turns
To balance, but the mind is slyer

And creeping from the caverned skull
Decisive thought's supremacy
Enforces in a moment strength,
But yet is served unwillingly.

VII

The melody, from treble tones
Of clarity and quick design,
Scaling the intervals descends,
Losing in overtones its line.
But still the listener will hear
The tune unchanging to his ear.

So in the personal unity
The intricate harmonies of mind,
Transposed to body, will become
Precision marred and undefined.
And yet the instrument contains
The tune; the single phrase remains.

To face the arrows of the chance-drawn bow,
To meet with equal gaze the shifting skies,
Is not so difficult for the fortressed mind.
But who wears armor 'gainst the civil foe?
And who, in desperate combat locked, can feel
Which self is true, which of the twin-born real?
How shall I choose between my hands, my eyes,
Secure a witchwand for the mind's pure spring?
Or how, unravelling the snarled threads, find
The single cord that frees me of my maze
Of self-evasions and of lost desiring?
Where is there peace among these tortuous ways;
Within is strife, without what meets my gaze?

IX

He who would be reborn must seek
The caverned stillness of the sea,
The liquid vaults where no new light
Has ever pricked the formless dark,
And antique slime yet bears the trace,
The smooth-worn mark of timeless self.

Like Aphrodite, he appears
And in the foamy revelry
Of sun-struck surface, reaches shore.

X: THE BLACK LEOPARD

O, stealthy beauty, crouching in my tree,
Concealed by patterned shadow on the branch!
Now satiation lies along your limbs,
And the slight movement of your latent strength
Is only visible in metric breath.
Silent, intent, parabola of might!
No one has seen you, hunting in the night,
Spring from your hiding, eager for the death
Within the scope of your extended claw.
I feel you stirring in the shade of sleep
And see your footprints trailed across my dream.
Reveal to me, you hieroglyph of night,
The meaning sheathed behind your metal eyes.

XI

Who sees the panic unconfessed,
The lightning in the quiet breast?
Even the lovers, closely clasped,
Know distance in their dual past.

Each in the furnace is annealed,
Enameled lips and eyes are sealed.
Each calls aloud, but who can hear?
His cry turns only to his ear.

And can you understand my words?
At your approach they flee like birds,
Timid of man; and for your part,
You hear the voice and not the heart.

XII

A sanctuary in a maze
Invisible to all who gaze,
Where polished leaves repel the sky
And in cool hiding love can lie.
There all hurt things can come to rest,
Where wounds are salved and sins confessed.

The inner chamber dark and hidden
To all clear seeing eyes forbidden,
A tomb concealing in its fear,
Worse than the dead, the empty bier.
The hunter waits and leashed his hound,
The silent watching for a sound.

My innermost identity
Is that which I most fear to see.

XIII

Within the spring's bright shell of dawn
The coming summer's hid.
Beyond the summer's burning noon
The autumn glaze is clear.
And when the copper evening falls
Then winter's night is soon.

But when the seasons cease to be,
When change no more endures,
The silence of eternity
Awaits no further sound,
Will there be endless night or day?
It matters not—by either way,
The awful instant, hard as death,
Requires neither thought nor breath.

Mould sprouts in old shoes and empty heads,
The formulary tree and shallow skies,
Refuse refurbished for the inadequate mind,
A place where melancholy multiplies.

The artists of this admirable scene,
The ticks and flies that batten on the sore,
Professionally mourning miserable deaths,
Declaim a dirge for what they do abhor,

Admitting in their threadworn threnody
No noble motive and no decent death
To present time, exhibiting decay
And thrice denying with their latest breath.

The past seen through a mirror is refined,
Simplified, cleansed, remarkably well-favored.
And in that past there was no fear, no doubt;
Their path was clear and their faith never wavered.

It is most difficult to hold the truth
That changes form and substance in your hand.
Must you deny that granite still exists,
Because your rock becomes a waste of sand?

XV

I do not know if you will know
The place to which I always go,
If you can trace upon the hill
The path I long to follow still,
Or track upon the tide-blank shore
My footsteps, where I walk no more.

I do not know if you will care
To follow me you know not where,
To pick an unfamiliar way
Through the stiffly rustling hay,
And climb with me the time-scarred rock,
And find the gate, and find the lock.

COLGATE DORR

Diana, mistress of the evening sky,
Immortal offspring of almighty Jove,
Attend my prayer. Thy temple fires burn high
That men may view the sacred olive grove
Where Leto crowned thee Lady of the moon,
The woods, the quiet glen, the grassy field.
Here thou wast taught to make the flowers bloom;
To drive the hunter's spear and lift his shield
Against the boar; and with thy light to guide
The lonely traveler on the midnight plain,
To show the trembling groom his naked bride,
And soothe the heavy womb far-stretched in pain.
And thou hast learned to fill the tree with fruit,
The fields with grain, the woods with fish and deer;
To measure out each month thy heavenly course
That men may watch thee pass and mark the year.
Long hallowed in the forest and the glade,
Long worshipped in the temple and the home,
Protect again the glories thou hast made,
The hills, the rivers, and the men of Rome.

However well a man may plan his days,
Still, circumstance, experience, and years
Bring in new elements and teach new fears.
What I have thought so firm, now fast decays.

The work I thought all Rome would surely praise—
That careful work, I cease, yet keep my tears.
Hard facts and age have taught that Roman peers
Must pass slow, mild, complaisant, careless days.

DONALD F. DRUMMOND

The meek inherit what we do not know,
Nor do the meek know that which they inherit:
But after every snow cloud comes the snow,
And after every mouse a hungry ferret:
The action in the form the actors show—
The meek inherit what, we do not know.

A pound of weight, a quart of size, a flow
Of oboe notes, a noose below a gibbet:
Each in itself seems what the measures show,
An opium dream an act which dreams prohibit.
Within the form the meaning's here below:
A pound of weight, a quart of size, a blow.

Upon these cortices the flickers grow,
The complex of the mind becomes remote.
And simple meekness, puzzled by the show—
Excess of judgment from the nervous throat—
In desperation sheds tomorrow's woe,
Nor do the meek inherit what we know.

The bird has flared his wingtips on the reef,
His beak extended like a whale boat prow;
And individual evil past belief
With caution teeters on the point of Now.
Gulls beyond sudden counting stiffly set
And tack their wings like cutters. In their glide—
The flash of wings above the flash of wet—
Is movement, universal as the tide.

No carrion taints that motion in the air.
No quick reflection lights these crusted eyes:
On the black reef I shun the knowing stare,
Seeking the separate principle which flies:
Between this only and those many birds
Lies ancient paradox escaping words.

How Sleep the Brave

*(An expedition of schoolgirls to the Hall
of Fame in the National Capitol Building)*

Although the words of men suffice
To deem them wise and name them great,
To make them heroes of the state
And fix their place in Paradise,

Although the noble words are said
And statues hammered, bronze or stone,
No memory of the perished tone
Contemns the bronzes of these dead.

Beneath that vast invested room
Where the great leaves of history fall
The human memory comes to call
Uncritical before the tomb.

And great grandchildren of the strong
Who fell at Breed's without a name
On tiptoe tread the Hall of Fame
Before the bust of Huey Long.

TO MY FATHER

The strong grow stronger in their faith
And from their strength their faith grows strong.
And you who fastened on a wraith
Which moved John Wesley were not wrong

To fix your being to that rock
From which the purest water flowed,
Allying pity to the stock
Whom Calvin fired into a goad

Which pricked old kings and cardinals
To fury, and whose faith subdued
The Plymouth winter, and the calls
Of flesh which tore the multitude,

Who built a solitary state
Upon the bare Laurentian soil,
Who looked on slothfulness with hate
That moment they were hating toil,

You were not wrong to scorn the man
Who scorning, turned the other cheek,
Nor with your grave religious scan
To seek the best which best men seek.

And you may challenge, not condemn
The risk each generation runs:
That faith from which your being stems
Prove insubstantial to your sons.

The elder boy I do not know:
    The dark eyes by the sun embossed
Record eight years, the structures grow,
    Who sees most clearly, most has lost.

The infant wailing in the dark,
    The nightmare of the early bed,
I hear no more; where is the mark
    They fastened in his eager head?

The tiny fingers grasped at Time
    Like a damp ring above a crib,
The scar is buried in the slime
    Where Adam lost another rib,

Where graying Priam heard the shout
    When Hector fell, or where the king
Found Absalom below the knout
    Of tangled hair. To name the thing

Which makes remote the root and flower,
    Sustaining variation won—
To name it Time arrests no hour,
    Grants me no boon to know my son.

Jenghiz upon the mountains white and high
Saw near a cliff a tiny frozen bird,
Then raised his sword and watched the Moslems die
Till not a single bloody body stirred.
Elizabeth spoke a poison-arrowed word
And Mary died beneath the headsman's hand,
And Pilate shunned the evidence he heard
To raise a Cross which shadowed Holy Land:

These by the Scorpion's touch, the queer Unplanned,
These by the headsman, governor, or Khan.
And no God makes the mighty understand
Why all of Satan's songs are undersung.
No Mercy tempers what the silence sheds
Upon the mighty in their lonely beds.

Epitaph for a Reno Woman

(For it is easier for a camel to go through a needle's eye, than for a rich man to enter into the kingdom of God.—St. Luke 18 : 25)

A pound of flesh, a pound of gold,
Are each my life, and each is old;
And neither worth the other's loss:
The heart needs gold to give it gloss
And no gold gleams without the Heart:
In each the other's counterpart.
And though rich women force that gate
They do not bear my double weight.

The great she-camel's stomachs swell:
She trots on madly by to hell.
And though I diet endlessly
My mind has fixed the width of me;
The narrow gate called Needle's Eye,
Exacts its penance, though I die:
For heaven gained, sans gold or touch
For two-humped beasts is not worth much.

She hung a pendant in between her breasts
Of platinum and jewels like sun through smoke.
She warmed the stones like redbirds in their nests.
The white and scented prison made one choke

For bitter beauty viewed with stiffened jaws
Through boundless terror into endless loss.
The symbol with the jewels in its claws
Was that of man spread-eagled on a cross.

In Rock Springs, snow beside the tracks
Lies gray from locomotive smoke.
The quick cold hems the yellow shacks
And covers that worn oxen yoke

Which lay across two labored necks,
Before the yellow shacks were built,
Which felt the quick cold in the flex
Of muscle over mud and silt

Where arrowheads of quartzite lay,
Before the oxen blundered by,
Containing cold each winter day
Since wind had blown the red blood dry

And fleshless lay the antelope
On hills which bore the absolute
Of absent warmth, which changed their slope,
Changed yoke and oxen and the brute

Who shot the arrowhead with hope,
And knew the hope die with its fall.
The cold endures the death of each,
Usurps the primacy of all,
Denies the fumbling power of speech.

Repository where the plane
Of page and line imprison thought
Although the past dies, one foot caught
Within the cloth-lined trap, the stain
Of tortured action must remain.

The stain impels the consequent
Tradition-hungry, overweight
Pursuer of the fleeing great
To stir the covers of event
Disturbing what the plane had meant

When hot and not benevolent
The words lay dripping on the page
Controlled above his love and rage
By what had been a cold intent
To suffer with the innocent.

The documented union of these hands
Authority has blessed with pomp refined
By countless unions; through the golden bands
The fingers slip, the flickering nervous kind,
The hardened digits of the dumb and slow
Suborned by ecstacy, the cynic's stem
Of cultivated scorn extended here
In genuflection to the law of man.

So to this altar came the scented head
Of Clytemnestra and her black-browed Greek,
Of Desdemona when the lacy bed
Extended generation to the meek,
Of Jezebel when Ahab knew his strength
Was born of God, and at her garment's hem,
Dissolved like salt; before they grew in fear—
Before the poison of the Will began.

Within this gray substantial rock
In changeless process heat and cold
Shear off the planes which interlock
Into a pyramidal mold:
Describe a mountain on a base
Whirling in speculative space.

Below the rock-slide lies this earth,
These particles of granite pan,
Providing victual for the birth
Of vegetable into man:
The fall of fragments like his bone
Is not determined by the stone.

The glint of quartz along the cleft
Of granite when the pieces fall
Provides a standard for the deft
Repair of cliff-face, that is all
Progression into utter doom
And changeless space within his tomb.

Caution

Beware, Aristotelian man;
Baal's bloody idols do not fall
By categories to your scan
And often tumble not at all.

Your catalog may not include
Twin rattlesnakes entwined below
A crown of porphyry: the crude
And polished art of Tezcuco.

The grim Dacotah waste of soul
Before a deer trapped in a pit
Writes nothing on your careful scroll,
Though death and madness come of it:

Empirical and evident
Are strength and motion, form and size:
None saw, when Samson's back was bent,
Intention in his mangled eyes.

The Word is framework where the Thing
    Finds boundaries, but the neatest sin
Applies the Word to weave a ring
    Where nothing may be bounded in

Or bounded out; the Spanish lord
    Converts the windmill into wind,
But no less graciously, the Board
    Of grey Directors, neatly pinned

By maps and charts, afford a glance
    At so much coal upon the wall
Or elevators crammed with chance
    And Kansas wheat. The pages fall

While grain is piled in burlap sacks,
    And each director drips with sweat:
The Thing discovers what it lacks
    That words have not discovered yet.

L. F. GERLACH

Nothing is gone, not time, when death is done.
The mind retraces what was scarce begun.
These are the lips, the eyes, the hands, the dust;
The life projected out of hope, and thrust
Back to the absolute and empty dreams,
The core that carried reflex to extremes.
A head, with logic stiff, retreats from thought,
But cannot lose the second self it wrought;
The mind must form no guilt—none can atone
For child that breathed but never came to bone,
For life that whimpered, sharp, spasmodic, red,
And, stilled, back through placental darkness fled.
What we prepared became another room.
Regret could not return death to the womb
To wait the proper time. The wish was done
Upon a bed where silence was begun.
The loss is old—this losing of a son.

From magistrate was bought
What we must dispossess.
The passage may be nought,

But has, as yet, not taught
The sufferance of "yes,"
The fortitude of nought;

A faith in fact it brought,
As one and one digress
To ever equal naught.

My margin is a fault of leaves
That breaks the rund'ling of these seasons;
The wild, confusing spring deceives
My ragged mind throughout the year
Till I recall, "Once there was rest."

Where is the granite hour will bear
Eternal absence of design?
In soaring windows through the dawn
Where men sleep, rigid, and resign,
Martyred, without infinity?

Among the clefts of wordless books
Which answer, "There are answers only"?
Among such faultless words as these?
Or hilled in silver Judas groves
Where will promotes its own disease?

Love is ever bought at best
For simple sounds of gratitude,
And all the heart that minds invest,
Enshrines a weary platitude.

The citied loss you bring or touch
Can never rouse what you are loving,
Though varnished faces shadow much
Of what decays in all your roving.

The glaze upon your visaged mind
May seal your sense, lead you to marry . . . .
If so, you'll find all womankind
A soothing Sanskrit dictionary,

Simple as a baker's thumb;
And having solved the white acrostic,
Your pride may be that you become
A shrewd, plucked ostrich or agnostic.

DEATH OF A TEACHER

To all to whom it now means nothing,
This was Jordan, this Keyserling,
And this Duhan—siftings in the mind,
Through sweepings of a rococo wind.

All in a year have now deserted;
Two in the ranked and sabered dead
Of scarred Silesia—and gray Duhan
Amid the candles bending down

Within their bright descending circles.
And light against the ceiling mulls
The wigged and mourning shadows in
Their whispering and braided satin.

Below, the rancid straw lies rotting,
Spread to muffle the grating and trotting
Of carriages passing, dark and indiscreet,
Over the brittle, frost-glazed street.

Behind the parted curtains of austerity,
At another window of Berlin—as great as he—
Stood Frederick's grief, his Prussian silence,
Not half so brilliant as his violence.

ANN LOUISE HAYES

He saw the wind diffuse soft dust,
     Subduing color to its glintless beige;
He watched the creek edge through the crust
     Of cracked gray earth which was its winter bed;
He touched stalks brittle with the drouth,
     And, propped against an unkempt, barren tree,
Savoured the hinting salt upon his mouth,
     Heard sea, spread thin on sand, reclaimed by sea.

Autumnal

Reaped is the harvest:
Only its stain
Purples my basket,
Fixed in its grain.

Marking indelible!
Yearly new dyes,
Seeped from new harvests
Compel my eyes.

Pale autumn daisies turn to face pale sun,
  Miscued by warmth to life too soon begun,
    Rising in frost-bent grass.

So thy too eager heart. Frost on the husk
  Warns of chill nights after the early dusk,
    Warns these bright days must pass.

Impatience brings but death: brave not the frost.
  Await thy rising in grass star flower tossed,
    Warmth will thy joys amass.

Aye, edge the trees in white,
  Promise the spring delight
    Warm sunlight limns.

Cover wet fields with green,
  Wild be the crops there seen,
    Sweet-wild and bright.

And hide the violets tossed
  Where watered rocks lie mossed—
    Profuse their screen.

Still, mind thy warmth condemns:
  Flowered and bare the stems,
    Nightly the frost.

Take thy silent entity apart,
  And watch the sure division of the heart
    Which, sleeping, strays.

Listen, in the quiet, to the mind
  Which consciousness no longer holds confined
    To reasoned ways

And hear thy sudden actions there absolved.
  Are wisdom then and longing not resolved
    But separate,

Each in its own dominion held from each?
  Discordant is all harmony we reach
    Or imitate

When half must be submerged that half may sound.
  O, would the heart could turn to wisdom found,
    However late!

POEM

Here poppies move beneath the sun
The brilliants of a spring begun,
The pledge of summer heat
Implicit in the heart's intent.
Yet cold must be the message meant
For, sunlit, they repeat
The challenge which a promise brings
To wait, throughout the quiet springs,
The summer when we meet.

POEM

They will not, then, with victory return.
　They cannot leave the winter or the sands
　　Nor come again to still the long concern.

Pray that they knew some purpose, saw an end,
　Believed the words, believed the lifted hands
　　Pointing a credo which their deaths defend.

IN DESCRIPTION

Full-spread the pointed leaf, bright-tipped the stalk
  As blossoms turn, leaning above the walk,
    Curved to the fading bricks by summer wind.

Answer the restlessness in gathering air!
  And leave the garden, the flowers waiting there,
    In hot perfume, waiting till rain shall find

And cool their tossing petals, and heat pass.
  Come lie upon the brittle, yellow grass
    Or climb the hill where digging wheels have lined

And rutted once, and now each stiffened crest
  Crumbles and breaks, its dust by weight compressed,
    Flattened and soft, yet packed and redesigned.

QUERY

Do hearts forget the wonder-sweet delight
    That first love brings?
Or do they turn through each remembering night

To lodge again in whispers day forgets?
    The moving leaves
Are small to take thy place with their regrets.

Weary with running long, though she is fleet,
She slides and stumbles. Mossy, wet, and cold
The ground to naked feet,

To Daphne, promised as Diana's maid,
In terror of Apollo's nearing hold.
O, now, alone, afraid,

She feels his fingers on her arm and hand,
And fails at last: though driven yet by fears
She can no longer stand.

His arms close on her even as she falls.
Her scream, despairing, far Peneus hears,
Him, rivergod, she calls,

Begging him come to save his child from harm.
She feels her father's overpowering aid
Within Apollo's arm:

Her body stiffens, bark encloses it,
Her face is lost in leaves; her feet are stayed,
In chilly earth are set

And rooted deep, growing as roots of trees.
"I meant to share my honour, I, divine,—
Laurel alone I seize.

"Oh yet, you fleeing nymph, I claim my own.
The leaves that hide you now I take as mine:
I pluck and twist my crown."

We cross sulphurous land
Where water turns its bed to orange and blue,
Transforming salty sand,
Although the water still is water's hue.

The air is cold but light
And filled with sun. From earth the heats arise,
Spreading to steamy height
Where geysers jet or boiling water lies.

The boards we stand on now
Protect us from the pool beneath our feet:
Its deepnesses I know
Cannot be measured, and I feel its heat.

Down in the darkest blue
The heat of water almost at the boil
Is concentrate. We view
The tiny sudden bubbles as they coil

And quickly, coiling, rise.
These do not break the surface they disturb;
But grown to bursting size
A mass of bubbles slowly lifts the curb

Of water's heaviness.
Rushing against the top, they burst to air—
They, hot and colorless,
Are turned to foam and water as we stare.

If quiet after music is more still
For sounds that linger yet within the air,
How quiet then the church: the bridal pair
Are met in echoes of processional.
Riches of grace be on them! For they will
To enter an estate that God made fair,
And humbly, in His presence Who was there
At rites in Cana, and did miracle.
Let quietness of marriage flow from grace,
With joy in doing that they ought to do,
With hope of God in all humility.
Let two be one, and in His sight embrace,
And in communion feel His love renew
God's blessing on them and His charity.

C. R. HOLMES

To John Fiorini

And now farewell, my friend:
the customary, few
well-chosen words might best
be uttered here, to lend

a proper dignity
to your familiar death;—
to grace this sunken cross
with formal piety.

In place of liturgy,
the empty, sterile chant
of acclimated words,
an island elegy

remains for you alone;
near-by the guns still roll
like thunder through the hills,
and hollowly intone

your unrequited end;
here silently I stand
before your sand-filled eyes,
and watch the slow waves mend

the shrapnel-wasted shore;
the curlews mince along
this scum-encircled beach
and nervously explore

the barbed and bloody wire:
not they, but rather I,
will one day hear with you
the abnegated choir.

You are prescient, near
me now, yet unexplained
by these cold words which fall
like dead birds round your bier.

ISLAND BATTLEFIELD

Perhaps some child was here,
    tired from its play,
and petulantly threw
    its toys away:

rag dolls left in the sun,
    on coral sands—
several toys pretend
    they have no hands.

The eyes are gone from one;
    another seems
still wholly formed, yet stirred
    by restless dreams;

and some have been too near
    the searching fires;—
smoldering dolls attest
    to coral pyres.

Leather handles gripped
by impartial hands;
separate from all
Palinurus stands

his accustomed watch;
guides the soot-flaked helm
with careless fingers
in the channeled realm;

quiets the screaming rails
with high-pressured air;
berths his yawing craft,
where the lank steels flare.

HOTEL LOBBY

The old men sit here, quietly lost,
each on a mottled, horsehair throne,
and mutter the songs of long ago,
songs without music, words alone.

Only the old men ever view
the frizzled sunlight's dusty track,
or watch the shadows play upon
a ceiling's frescoed bric-a-brac.

It pleases old men to recall
their patient, half-forgotten dreams,
that linger like the nap-frayed rug,
stamped patternless, with rotting seams.

The resting blood that once would run
its hurried course through upswept loins
is thinned and joined in apathy
with ancient, desiccated groins.

On borrowed time, in borrowed chairs,
these breathing dead in ordered ranks
sit endless watch and only stir
to ease their acclimated flanks.

Included, European plan:
one potted plant per chair plus sand;
one fringe of slow-decaying life,
plus Death near-by each blue-veined hand.

Old faces in a gambling hall,
like fluid clouds of smoke released
yet bound to hang volitionless,
and pointless as an ugly scrawl.

Tired bodies limp with venal sloth,—
these patriarchs of Sodom knead
with dying sexuality
the dry, green, checkered folds of cloth.

For long they watch the stumbling flights
of ivories cast across the boards;
these turn their pock-marked faces up
in deference to the acolytes.

The rooted, ancient women stayed
in whalebone, pink elastic bands,
are greying penguins come to trough,—
septic sensualists betrayed.

Within the truss, behind the glasses,
stands First Genie, Former Master,
Past Exalted, Wizard Knighted,
Virtue Errant for the masses.

All music is the sound of gears,
meshing in oil and murmuring,
yet thunderous when coins applaud
each degradation of the years:

For these are Fortune's elder slaves,
in mixed pursuit of alien ways;
come to abet the violation
of their patient, fallow graves.

Abandoned Brothel

Bordello squatting motionless,
whose flaccid awning idly views
the city traffic coalesce
and grind ahead in rocking queues.

Venetian blinds in ambuscade
for cleft, infiltrating sunlight,
your rooms are deeply glossed with shade
where sleeps the day's inverted night.

The chairs are stern, inviolate;
arraigned in rows, each hunchback seems
an arrogant sophisticate—
companionless, immersed in dreams.

Deserted brothel, made apart
from human prayer and left alone;
so wearied of the elder art
of desiccated love on loan.

"Gentlemen in the parlor, girls!"
—lost echoes frantic in the gloom—
stand, smile, and pat the hennaed curls,
and, yawning, walk into the room . . . .

MELANIE HYMAN

What forms of anguish might this pattern show
If men, who wisdom praise, the wise disown?
The more I understand, the more I know,
The more it seems that I become alone.
Since I, for words I held the truth, have wept
For love and friendship I no more possess,
Then loneliness I early shall accept,
That sooner I can live with loneliness
Finding in him such gentle company
That I'll not be despite events of men
Wholly deserted. Now you go from me
Your going must not cause me pain again.
　　What bitter cheer—if trials to come have only
　　The hope of finding ease in being lonely.

BALANCE

There dropped a leaf upon my hand,
A friendly touch to look and feel
The beauty of the summer land—
The lake's dry place, light green and teal,
Where shadows fronted bordering trees;
The very peace and quietness
Were then a source of happiness.

Not always thus, my soul can rest.
I've fancied in my darkest days,
To break the thread off early lest
Grief come in worse and unknown ways.
But bitterness new value gave;
Those thoughts of death made life more sweet
Since death and life one whole complete.

We veterans of babes' diseases,
Fire, flood, smothering, chance misfortune,
War's destruction, crime increases,
Starving, still-birth, and abortion,
Though survival's been our portion,
Risk it when we play, or drive.
Death is near while we're alive.

We, who have seen the grief in life
Enough to see the good in death,
May be consoled: though sweets of life
We lose, grief also ends with breath.
For with this wisdom life on earth
Can be, not clung to fearfully,
But held with calm serenity.

HELEN PINKERTON

In touching gently like a golden finger,
The sunlight, falling from the spaces dimmer
Upon the curling fruit leaves, fills with hunger
The mind, for meaning, in the limpid summer.

Dispersed by myriad surfaces in falling,
Drawn into green and into air dissolving,
Light is not caught by sudden sight or feeling.
Remembered it gives rise to one's believing

Its truth resides in constant speed descending;
The momentary beauty is attendant.
A flicker of the animate responding
Shifts in the mind with time and fades, inconstant.

Green growing bush, compounded elements,
The clean excrescence of the earth, the first
To rift the stony desert face and burst
The rigid outline with a foliage dense,
Your latest leaf against my garden fence
Is older than the silent man you nursed;
But silent too with only mortal thirst—
Is younger than the man whom man invents.

Your budding and fruition do not wait
For man; you are more sure of pace than he
Who would of you a verity create,
A measure of his own inconstancy,
Take you from silence as a speaking mate
To share his passage to eternity.

SUBJECTIVITY

I measure years by days and days by hours
But in the elastic hour of calculation
I leave immeasurable the instrument.
In my delineations watches bend,
The slow distortion of amorphousness,
And now the bullet's flight may be the moth's
When, simultaneously, I ride with both.
No frozen age, no night perpetual
On Georgian steppes and canyons of the west,
When a dead moon reflects a dying sun,
Turning to the unheard refrains of time,
Is longer, darker, than the eyelid's rest,
The veil of flesh before oblivion.

Two Sonnets: *To a Spiritual Entity*

I

I did not see you even when I went
From the long afternoon's forgetfulness
Into a night of knowing the distress
Of questioning your presence and intent.
If you I look for when my discontent
Is more than tentative unhappiness
Are not the mere reply of mind in stress,
Be with me casual and concomitant
As gentle breathing in a midnight sleep
When no one bids the breast to rise and fall.
Be as a quiet fire of which I keep
The welling warmth in blood the veins recall
When love, released from too much freedom, tries
The film of cold on hands and lips and eyes.

II

If I had stood, waiting for you to come,
Expecting your arrival momently
With bells and horns, the sounding of a drum—
All the mechanic signs of victory—
Of course I had deceived myself, because
I knew that I must travel to the end
Of me, departing thence to that which was
No part of me. When I could still contend
"Perhaps you will not be there," I could pause
Always before the word that you prescribe
And fail to find you. For, though you, the same
Who waits upon the border, circumscribe
Infinity, denial in me was
Infinity and bore a different name.

Rest on this shore, Aeneas, for a time.
Your restlessness intent upon new Troy
Fans pride to ardency, while love, of which
You are the temple, guttering, spends no heat
In indolent and generous persuasion
To love and let ambition's tumult die.
The shores Fate promised you and where in dreams
Your father goads you, flee, as he, your hand.
I am as much Lavinia as she
Who waits a husband at her father's side,
Only unsanctioned by your father's house
And by Apollo's word, I am forbidden
And all my sweetness, bitterness to you.
Your willingness alone, not prophecies
Of men or gods' commands shall say which shore
Will be your end, and you consented once
When we two hid together in the cave.
You need say neither yes nor no. Your ships
And men will never leave without your word
And no word will, to me, mean your consent.
Remember Troy's defeat. I think you know
No man has built a city to withstand
The long and individual years and wars.
But you could find in me a changeless love.
Which do you long for: rest or restlessness?
Do I see only part of you or do
I see more than you see yourself and know
The hidden truth: that fear not courage drives you
Journeying nether seas, that vanity
Not love demands for your Ascanius
A heritage of lands and high-born name?
Your naked body is your own, but you
Choose to engreave it by an iron will,
To jacket it with brass that glints and knots,
Each act repeating known act, till the form
Fit you as armor and as intricately.
How can the idol be complete, the image
Lucid and still embodied in the flesh
When none of what is flesh and blood is clear
And only tissued with illusive form?
I have no wisdom and no tongue to leap
The edge of mind and lash you to myself.

Words crumble in my mouth, I cannot reason.
Inactive here in Carthage I must wait
Your spirit's acquiescence, as the sea
With liquid tongues of force must wait in patience
Your body's dissolution on the shore.

Father, I fear your love,
When I remember wisdom I once knew
And strength and freedom in the movement of
My willing thoughts to you.

A sweet dependency.
Love was the loadstone meaning hung upon,
Till reason's weight sprung the periphery.
Simplicity is gone.

My way is past retreat.
Love's roots known, they support that faith no more,
But I may be deceived and still complete
Your fiat as before.

Revolt, as fealty,
Is ruled by love, but love—to live—commands
Its own obedience to a deputy,
The will which understands.

W. WESLEY TRIMPI

LEDA

Leda release
The sensuous swan;
A god's caprice
Is quickly gone.

Through tangled reeds
The bird again
Slowly recedes
Into his brain.

Thy loins still tremble.
Behind thy stare
Thy mind must dissemble
His presence there.

The cleavage lies
Where the unknown
Fills the disguise
Of flesh and bone.

The wall, a bony finger,
    Points away
From land while sea gulls linger
    White and gray
And black upon the air.

Sometimes a fish is trapped;
    It jumps and flings
Thin circles overlapped,
    Expanding rings
From which the waters stare.

The estuary sleeps;
    The ocean like
A giant rodent creeps
    Along the dike
And licks the surface bare.

ASTERIA

Born of a star, they say,
    You dropped to sea,
    Though now you stay
    In foliage
    With grass and tree
    For heritage.

Take from the star your name,
    For few will know
    You are the same
    Who fled from Zeus
    And flew below
    The Heaven's loose

And ranging floor, a girl
    Transformed into
    A quail to hurl
    Herself from him
    From whom she flew.
    But now each limb

Again has changed itself:
    Your breast now lies
    A sandy shelf,
    An island hull,
    Where nests and dies
    The mortal gull:

Your bones now hold the hills;
    Turned stone, they make
    The dikes and sills
    Beneath the earth;
    The shallow lake,
    Which streams gave birth,

Lies inland from the shore:
    And now your feathers
    On the tor
    For mile on mile
    Have bred the heathers
    Of the isle.

SILENT PIANO

She left the keys and dropped
Some yellow music back
Into the bench; though, propped
Against the music rack,
Open to where she stopped,
Some stays like bric-a-brac.

The strutting hammers rest
In motionless quadrille;
The tripled strings are pressed
Across the framework grill,
Like vessel cables stressed
At anchor, taut and still.

The black mahogany,
Where cavern tones are bred
Of peace or agony,
Is now a coffin spread
With casket ebony,
And all its sounds are dead.

The idols of the mind
Are thought and heart and will;
Their semblance makes us blind
To functions they fulfill;
Though each can be defined,
We shall confound them still.

Pygmalion conceived
The perfect love in thought.
In ivory he achieved
The lover that he sought,
And yet he was deceived:
It was himself he wrought.

The pared marmorean mass,
Becoming flesh from art,
Whose soul's incestuous glass
Reflects its counterpart,
Assumes an alias
Of spirit and of heart.

And thus is Paphus bred:
Two bodies and one soul
Create a spirit dead,
Although the flesh be whole,
And circumstance has led
Beyond the mind's control.

ELEGY

Forgotten playground, grave
  Of children's joys,
Decay in silence save
  For crickets' noise
    Continuous.

Your iron bars wear moss
  In rusty flakes
And crudely form a cross,
  Like unnamed stakes
    Incongruous.

They soon will fall away
  And disappear
Beneath the summer's hay,
  Nor reappear
    Again to us.

SONNET

The mole, which sleeps beneath the woven peat,
Is not awakened by the blinding day;
Now caught beneath the hot and musty hay,
It cannot ever see the freshening wheat
Where creeps the cool canal on hidden feet
And where the willows hide the dusty way,
When Spring finds Summer's bode in finding May.
So degradation has a last retreat,
A sounding place which has no counterpart;
To hide itself, yet still to vilify,
From mind, from act it slips into the heart:
Once there it gazes with a sightless eye,
And there, inert where crimson channels start,
It cannot live, yet cannot ever die.

The beggar does not sulk in grime
To be complete like other men;
Hideous doll in pantomime
Of ugliness, he shows his den

To those who pass; they see his limbs,
His legs are scarcely one foot long.
He finds no rest in peaceful hymns,
Nor in the cricket's lonely song.

They drop the money in his pan.
I thought, is he perhaps a child
Now reincarnate from a man
Whose own existence was defiled.

His eyes, like coals on paraffin,
Melt through his face; his wordless tongue
Implies pale gratitude from thin
Icteric lips; his teeth are strung

Beneath like small misshapen beads
Across his jaws; his twisted nail
Is like the birds' that scratch for seeds
In arid lands worn smooth and pale.

Affliction is affliction's shield,
A shield which no one will condone;
Distress within itself is healed,
And misery must stand alone.

He measures time in misery
Till flesh will grow, or will decay;
Till he be more complete than we,
Or till all flesh shall fall away.

The glass swan treads the shining water
Of the crystal table. Strange,
She moves the way the dancers taught her,
Moving as her colors change.

Behind her women pass in red
And gold and drop upon her back
The tints which through her body spread
A flush of yellow, blue, and black.

The movements cease; she hesitates
In white beside a woman's hand,
And with an emerald eye she waits
And looks upon the silver land.

She watches till the music starts,
Closes her eyes, and then departs.

The body is not spent;
The mind is complement
To but a little lust:
We do but what we must.
Our only will is want,
And it is sheathed in gaunt,
Complacent gauze of flesh,
Alive nor full nor fresh.
The mind is but a waste
Of thought, inert, defaced;
And doubt, the slow dissembling
Loss of intent, the trembling
Choice without willing choice,
Echoes illusion's voice.

To Orpheus

Your lyre became your voice,
Denied by all until
Pluto perceived the soft
Compulsion of your will.

But impulse made you turn
And lose her, fading back
Into eternal wastes,
Unsought and without track,

While reason shuddered at
Unmeaning forms, as they
Appeared, diffused, and, shade
By shade, they passed away.

The lust of mind is pride,
Insatiate, not to hide,
Whose cold, insensuous touch
My hand has felt too much.
Discriminations grow
Too fine for what I know
And formulate privation
In intricate evasion.

Though judgment be astute,
Man has no absolute
Except what he has sought,
Chiselled and cold, in thought.
Spun through his indecision
By infinite revision,
Dependence thus denied,
His will grows into pride.

What then shall take the place
Of pride? I know no grace
To follow or invent
To ease my discontent;
And though I may be sure
Illusion is secure,
I know not what I am,
And all my pride is sham.

Interminable contingency,
Impending and immediate,
Yours is the touch I almost flee
And almost seem to consummate.

Finality is so severe:
Unknowing and remorse repeat
An old irrevocable fear
Which leaves intention incomplete.

Still mutable and still afraid
To move beyond what I can know,
I seek to be what I evade
In terror of becoming so.

Sired by Zeus in a barren tower, unseen
And without sound, out of a sudden blaze
Perseus was conceived. On the granite floor
Mother and infant trembled in the cold:
Dreaming, she saw in the god's wide sunfilled eyes
Europa lashing the white bull's back and Leda
Dazed by the furious strokes of the swan's white wings.
Perseus, fathered by a god, half-brother
To Helen and Minos, cried the Delphic curse
Not to himself but to Acrisius
Who sought to drown his daughter and her child.

Swung in the cold swell of an empty sea,
Conducted to a shore, rocky and foreign
Beneath a wash-cut slope where shrunken cattle
Sought the sparse grass, they found another home
And another king. Perseus grew till perception
Became his growth; but, unwilling to discern
Where certainty was solitude, he lived,
Rude and idle in the ignorant household
Of an imperceptive king. But Polydectes,
Fearing corruption less than loneliness,
Banished him from an inarticulate kingdom
And left him speechless in the trade of a crowded coast.

Athena, goddess of wisdom, and Hermes, shrewd
Friend of Charon, inventor and magician,
Found him in broken hills and showed him the gifts
Of the nymphs: the winged sandals and magic pouch,
And Pluto's ghostly helmet. Perseus followed
Across the stubble, into the fields of wheat
And barley where brown flights of tiny birds
Burst from the grain and vanished like his thoughts,
Caught momentarily in the mind, and lost—
And yet he knew the birds would flush again.
He saw and knew, and yet perceived that there
Were things he could not see, nor ever know.

In Libya he found the Gorgon temple
That he sought. Mingled with the hiss of sand,
The soft reptilian anger spread to meet him
Through the pillared courts. Medusa sat alone,
The visible finality of sense:
Beyond her lay a wilderness of stone
As incorporeal as death in the haze
Of the desert heat. Perseus murdered her,
And knew he could not look beyond his glass:
Hard with intent, he watched the emerald heads
Plunge and lift in her deep fuliginous eyes.

PEARCE YOUNG

EXHORTATION

Grow no older than your fears
And swear that time will never blind
That true proportion of the mind
Which seals the tumult of the years.

And swear that doubt will never heal
In dry consent to easy mirth,
That still the rude untutored earth
May know the harrow and the steel.

But if in time the false refrains,
The purling psaltery of the crowd
Unnerves the will which hope endowed
Or steals the grace your love contains,

Then pray that mind may still invest
Its little passion with the dust,
And turning from the motes of lust,
May win its season or its rest.

The evening bends upon a stubborn day.
Across the wind and sea the ages ride
And tumble to a surf where sea gulls play
Amid erupted fossils of the tide.
Unbowed within his milligram of space,
Each man who wanders on the darkening strand
Affirms the first inception of the race
From ancient signs far littered on the sand.

For time has measured well, and now the mind
May speak with certainty of older souls
Untended by the questions of mankind.
And man like grey and jutting stone may sleep
Amid the shocks and whispers of the deep
While ashen gulls turn seaward from the shoals.

THE WINTER FLOOD

*(Written upon the burning of a Negro's
home in Redwood City, California)*

The day assembles through a broken sky.
Our sleep and winter slowness in the blood
Provide convenient reasons for our sloth,
And crime, though old and master of the flood
And straining still to mastery of the mind,
But faintly stirs remembrance of our hate.
The season dumbly cancels all our debts.
The day is not unusual, only late.

And here within this day, like other days
Or years remembered cold in retrospect,
A slight disturbance in the winter air
Is little cause to pity or reflect
That sin is common still and still unbound.
Tomorrow there are duties to fulfill
And sleep has rusty wings to bear our fame
To higher reaches than the feeble will.

And thus inured and sealed within ourselves,
We turn from grief as travelers turn from lands
Unpleased with common air and common speech.
Today our dull obliquity demands
But little more than shame or cheap chagrin
That race cannot be reconciled with race.
The killer, swift and strong upon the night,
Is cause for terror in a foreign place.

For mind itself is lost to flood and crime.
Nor has the sleep of reason yet bestowed
A gentleness to fate or proved that we
Are more than figures on a dusty road.
Alone, and unprotected by a faith,
The holy bow before the public mind,
And since compassion is a costly thing,
Indifference appears to heal mankind.

To hope that wisdom may return to man,
That yet the crippled animal may find
The reasons for his fate beyond the land,
Is peace and pleasant pasture for the mind;
But hope cannot be fed beyond desire,
And lost, desire now weary of the chase
Is willing to accept the winter flood
And call upon illusion's ready face.

AT THE GRAVE OF MY GRANDFATHER

The years I knew you cannot grow
Beyond the structure of the bone.
A rule of memory rules disguise,
And where this little passion lies,
Intent has hardened to a stone,
Obscuring all that I have known.

This cold inscription has not placed
Authority upon the lime.
Old waters flow beneath your grave;
The tender laws you hoped to save,
Like peace, are catalogued in time,
And earth alone can know your waste.

By vigilance some minds may keep
The gentle music they possess,
But lute and lyre cannot impress
An age grown monstrous in its sleep.

For here our newer wisdom stands
Unchartered in a world of change.
Here is a darkness we must range.
No music grows within these lands.

O still your hopes! Let anguish wear
Its russet colors to the grave.
No drowsy winter king may save
His falling empire from despair.

Let love grown cold and hard mistrust
The tawdry rhythms of the race
Till quietude and time replace
These arid seasons of disgust.

Old age has scattered disbelief
In broken seeds behind new plows,
And doubt, once lost beyond belief
Now intersects his vows:

Here reason lies, its strength disposed,
Blind matter to the toil of mind.
Grey symbols test; the will is posed,
Dissected and defined.

And passion is the reckless weed,
Untended, sprawling, tough as wire.
Its tendrils reach unholy seed,
A polyp of desire.

Cold solace that the hills remain
When steely winds have sheared the green.
The shallow concept in the brain
Lies studied and foreseen.

No clashing arms, no wounds to hide,
No burning rood nor angry creed.
With stiff and automatic pride
He hungers where the hungry feed.

To a Giant Sequoia, Fallen and Enshrined in Calaveras County, California

An old infirmity has left its traces.
Sad with motion, fecundity and birth,
Even ages tired of your embraces.
Calmness turned to darkness and to earth.

Speechless to the wind, diurnal races
Once grew beyond your power to define.
Destruction out of time has measured worth.
Indefinite cause has managed your design.

Ten thousand years have left but little waste.
You lie, not sovereign to a new demesne
But as a ruin which death has somehow graced
With gradual passages of denser green.

A longer sickness is the mind's expense
In testing reasons for your eminence.

Now quietly the evening tends
The forces active in the brain.
Without, a patterned world extends.
Beyond the window, measured rain.
Within, the mystery of light
Is part of passion in the bright
Old world of hope where peace descends.

Here lie two latitudes combined:
Though in the high ebb of the blood
Gross action strains upon the flood
Of new desire, within the mind
The old world has her wonders still,
Her island solitudes behind
Her angry weather and her hills.

The fire burns low; the charred logs fall;
Grey ashes sift between the grates.
And all is borrowed, love and all
Like borrowed warmth regenerates
The quiet hope, the faint surmise
Which tells the hand the smooth wood lies
Like certainty, below its weight.

While yet in time our last intent
May single wisdom as its prize,
Will is a fleshy thing that lies
Within the hush of sacrament.

For those whose house is built of flesh
Must bear the ghosts within its halls.
Age is a night where grey snow falls.
Within this house the soul must thresh.

O youth, what frail security
Persuasions of the blood allow!
A little while may teach us how
To turn and doubt your majesty.

In time, in time our willful race
May learn some secrets from the dead,
But wild is wine and fierce is bread
And wisdom is a quiet place.

But now a little while is Time,
And Time itself is very long.
The ghosts are speechless to the strong.
The house is holy in its crime.

OCTOBER GARDEN

This blaze of leaves, your hand
Extended here to mark
The flight of birds, the band
Of yellow light, the arc
Of bees against the blue
Periphery of sky,
Ascribe all angles to
Perfection in the view.
No loose arrangements vie
With pleasures of the eye.

Yet here where all is ease,
Confused within the mind,
A world of yellow bees
Disintegrates all lined
And perfect lucid schemes.
The sun in passing seems
The light that first began
Within old Adam's eyes,
Those eyes that could not scan
The vertigo of dark.

And all will come to this:
The shadow and the bright.
No logic can dismiss
The burning in the light.
Intense and blind, the fruit
May fall, gaining some gay
Momentum in the mute
Explosion of the day.
Earth reasons for its all,
Absorbing there its fall.

For this is all: the deep
Grown pleasure of the day,
Waiting for age, the sweep
Of yellow gone to grey
Exhaustion as the slow
October mounts to rain.
And what you thought secured,
The closed geometry
Of your intent will be
Half-kept, like love endured
To winter and the snow.

Within these walls of rustic wood
The cloying scents of heaven cling.
Now turned to prayer they seek to bring
The injured world to brotherhood.

With hallowed words the weary ban
Of grief repairs, and in the rude
Rejoicing night the certitude
Of God returns to mind of man.

And here, they vow, their village Christ,
Home from his fields and troubled kine,
Will feed his flocks with virgin wine
And call them up to paradise.

But if this Christ, like temperate rain
Renews their earth, yet while they sleep,
A famine may destroy their sheep
And spoil the mellow resting grain.

O cold and studied doubt! The eyes
Have conjured up their tears again.
The hungry winter waits for rain.
In fields the yellow stubble dies.

And hope alone may comfort you,
But proud and dying like the year
It searches far for signs and blear
Disfigured landscapes scar the view.

O House of God! Still envied place!
Now blind and dumb, the faithful herd
Perpetuate the wavering word
And damn the cold bewildered race.

A Litany for Peace

The cold ideal
That mind selects
And love perfects,
Draws no appeal.
New fashion censures
Our old indentures.

And peace regained
Through values lost
Involves a cost
To be sustained.
Our vows once spoken
Receive no token.

Though time protests
No love endures,
That peace secures
Unwanted guests,
There is a slumber
That we may number.

A time when mind
May break the last
Unwilling fast.
In ages find
A sweeter potion
For its devotion.